# ETSY

# Open an Etsy Storefront and Launch Your Handmade Empire

# BOOK DESCRIPTION

Etsy is a global marketplace where craft entrepreneurs make millions of dollars by selling handmade crafts and vintage products. If you are talented or skilled in do-it-yourself handmade crafts or you have access to such skills and products, then, Etsy is the place for you.

This book provides you with information on how to open an Etsy storefront and launch your handmade empire. Etsy is a multibillion-dollar marketplace where a budding entrepreneur can start, grow and scale up enough to take up a significant share of these billions. There are those who have made this giant success, nothing can stop you. All you need is information on how to achieve this huge success. It is this information that we are providing to you in this book.

Scaling up your business and automating it is what will grow your empire and differentiate it from small-scale trades. No one starts a business with the aim of remaining stagnant and struggling just to earn barely sustainable profits. You will obviously want to reach a level where the business works for you. Scaling up and automation is the secret to let your business work for you, not you work for it. In this book, you will find all the information you need to scale up and automate your Etsy business so that your small business grows into a big handmade crafts empire like all other empires that began small.

Get this book and learn more.

# GIFT INCLUDED

If you are an entrepreneur, an aspiring entrepreneur, someone who is trying to create additional income stream or even someone who just loves self-improvement books; then you need to read my recommendations for top 10 business books ever. These books read by me have changed my life for the better.

Top 10 Business Books

# ABOUT THE AUTHOR

George Pain is an entrepreneur, author and business consultant. He specializes in setting up online businesses from scratch, investment income strategies and global mobility solutions. He has successfully built several businesses from the ground up and is excited to share his knowledge with you. Here is a list of his books.

<u>Books of George Pain</u>

# DISCLAIMER

# CONTENTS

# INTRODUCTION

The difference between a handmade and machine-made craft is the difference between a human handshake and a robot's handshake.

People world-over increasingly desire to have authentic handmade crafts where they can feel the touch of a human hand. They want to reconnect with the world that the machine has robbed from them – the network of human touch. Etsy is a community where this human touch is made possible, in not only buying and selling handmade crafts but also engaging with other community members about the feel of this human creativity.

This book provides you with information that can help you, the creative entrepreneur, extend your "handshake" to the rest of humanity through the creative power of your handmade crafts. The platform to do so already exists. The community is already there. All you need is to understand 'HOW!'

Keep reading!

# WHAT IS ETSY?

Etsy is the world's biggest online community marketplace for craftwork. It is a global community where creative minds express and exchange value for their intrinsically creative solutions using marketing tools.

**The nature of Etsy**

Etsy is:

- a community of creative people interacting and expressing their creativity
- a marketplace where creative people gather to exchange value in creative solutions
- an e-commerce platform with tools that facilitate the exchange of creative value

**The nature of creative solutions**

Well, at Etsy, you will find different sorts of craftwork. These are the goods on the displayed on the marketplace. They become products when they are blended with a unique service that cannot be isolated from the good itself. These products transform into a solution when they trigger an inert desire in those who visit the marketplace and adequately satisfy that desire in both intrinsic and extrinsic terms.

## Types of creative solutions

There are two main types of creative solutions available on Etsy:

- Handmade crafts
- Vintage crafts

## Handmade crafts

These are non-manufactured crafts. They are made through work of one's creative hands as an expression of one's creative idea.

## Vintage crafts

Etsy considers a product as vintage only if it is at least 20 years old.

## Parties to Etsy's creative solutions

There are three main types of parties on Etsy:

1. Creative collectors (creative buyers)
2. Creative marketers (creative sellers)
3. Creative facilitator (creative platform)

## The origin of Etsy

Etsy was born in 2005 by Ionspace. Ionspace itself is a brainchild of Robert Kalin, Chris Maguire, and Haim Schoppik. It is Kalin who baptized baby 'Etsy' ("eh, si"). In Latin, this translates to "oh, yes", while in French, it translates to "what if?" Well, maybe we can creatively blend the two meanings to come up with our own - "What if? Oh, yes!"

What if we can meet online to exchange our creative value through the work of our hands so as to meet our inner desires? Oh, yes! Etsy! And so Etsy was born.

**Etsy's main features**

Etsy has three main features:

1. Community
2. Marketplace
3. Platform

**Community**

Etsy is a membership-based community where those who intend to exchange value (creative collectors and creative marketers) have to register in order to make it possible for this creative process to take place.

**Marketplace**

A marketplace is where buyers and sellers come to exchange value. Thus, it is a place where buying and selling take place. We can explore these selling and buying features:

Selling

To become a seller on Etsy marketplace and thus be able to provide your creative solutions, you will need to open an account, create a username and, optionally but importantly, creatively brand your shop.

It is free to open and brand your shop on Etsy marketplace. However, you will pay a charge of $0.20 per listing valid for a 4-months duration, subject to renewal.

Whenever you make a sale, Etsy will claim 3.5% of the sales price, being the cost and reward of maintaining the platform that serves the marketplace. However, the billing is done only monthly basis with a 15-day grace period within which to pay.

Etsy marketplace also avails shipping options should you need to ship to a customer. The shipping options are billed separately and based on the seller-shipper agreement.

Buying

Etsy platform has an intuitive search engine that makes it easy for buyers to search for creative solutions to fit their wants. A buyer can search with precision by typing the name of the item on the search bar. Alternatively, the buyer can filter categories, make a further filter based on the sub-categories that pop-up, and eventually pick the desired item from the list of items that emerge.

Some of the common categories to search from include:

- Art
- Jewelry
- Vintage
- Home and Living
- Women
- Kids
- Men
- Gift Ideas
- Crafts supplies
- Mobile accessories
- Trending Items
- Etc...

Once the shopper finds the right item, she selects the particular item and click 'Add to Cart' so that the items are added to the shopping cart. The shopper can add as many items as the purchasing power can allow. Once finished adding items to the cart, the buyer can then proceed to make payments.

There are several payment options. The following payment options are allowed:

- Credit/Debit Card
- PayPal

**Benefits of establishing a shop and selling on Etsy**

The following are the most important benefits of establishing your shop on Etsy:

- Very simple and intuitive platform that aids the set-up process
- Non-technical approach to getting started
- A large number of buyers in the market
- Large exposure potential customers due to high customer traffic in Etsy marketplace
- Extremely cheap to get started

# SHOULD YOU SELL ON ETSY?

Making the decision to sell in any given marketplace is determined by several factors. The following are the most prominent of them:

1. Accessibility to the market
2. Potential of finding buyers
3. The probability of making a profit
4. Business sustainability and growth prospects

Let us explore each of these factors with regard to Etsy marketplace.

**Market accessibility on Etsy**

Market accessibility is determined by the following key factors:

- Nature of products saleable on the market – Etsy market is for creative products, primarily handmade crafts.
- Ease of entry – Etsy platform has been created keeping in mind the utmost simplicity. It is so easy to create a business account, create a shop and brand it, list your products and market them.
- Cost of establishing a point of sale – A point of sale on Etsy is one's listing. It only costs $0.20 to create a listing. Yet, the platform is such intuitive to make it less costly in terms

of time and effort required to create a listing. There are plenty of tools at your disposal just to make it as effortless as possible.

- Stock-holding capacity – You can list as many products as you can, provided that you stick to the nature of products allowed on Etsy (that is, handmade products and vintage products). How much you can keep as stock depends on the existing and potential demand. It also depends on the cost of acquiring and storing the stock.

- Delivery capacity – When it comes to delivery, Etsy does not limit you. It has enough facility on its platform to enable you to execute a delivery transaction. You are free to make your own arrangements as to how to ship the products being delivered. Nonetheless, Etsy has several shipping solutions from which you can choose.

- Payment capacity – Etsy offers various local and international payment solutions. You can be paid via credit/debit cards, PayPal, among other popular means of payment. However, PayPal is the default mode of payment.

# Potential for finding buyers on Etsy

The following factors determine the potential of finding buyers of your solution in a given marketplace:

- The volume of buyers – Etsy has had 33.4 million buyers over a period of less than a decade. There are several millions of buyers each year. The good thing is that Etsy does not restrict you from advertising elsewhere for buyers to visit your shop. Thus, apart from the millions of buyers within the Etsy's own ecosystem, you can still tap into the billions of potential buyers across the internet.

- Buyers' purchasing power – The advantage Etsy being a more specialized marketplace is that most potential buyers who come to Etsy are people who are looking creatively authentic handmade products. These are buyers with relatively higher purchasing power compared to those who would go for cheaper manufactured products. Moneywise, Etsy has been able to register positive growth in billions of revenue, which is a pointer to the fact that most buyers visiting the marketplace have sufficient purchasing power to drive these billions.

- Matching buyer persona – The hardest part for any seller is to predict the potential buyer persona. However, with Etsy being a highly specialized market, this work is drastically reduced. There are sufficient statistics about the marketplace which Etsy itself provide that can enable you to establish your potential buyer persona and create matching products to it. It is not as hard as determining the same on a general marketplace such as eBay and Etsy.

**The probability of making profits on Etsy**

The following factors determine the potential for making profits in any given marketplace:

- The cost of bringing products to the market – Other than the costs of shipping, there is a minimal cost of bringing your products to Etsy marketplace. In actual practice, what you bring to Etsy marketplace is the information about your products. Your physical products are in your own inventory, not in Etsy stores. Thus, you do not incur shipping costs unless the product has been bought. In this case, the buyer funds the shipping cost as part of the selling price. What is important is to ensure that you make appropriate costing so that all costs are reflected in the selling price so that you do not incur losses.

- The cost of selling – The cost of selling refers to that cost incurred in the marketplace in terms of finding a buyer, making a deal with the buyer and closing the deal. At the bare minimum, this cost is simply $0.20 + 3.5\%$. That is, the cost of listing plus Etsy's sales commission (of making a deal with the buyer and closing the sale on your behalf). Other than that, the other cost you probably would need to incur is the cost of branding and advertising.

- The cost of payment processing – Payment transaction cost depends on your chosen method of payment. This includes the cost of currency conversion (if your local currency is not US Dollar), processing fee by the payment gateway (Visa/MasterCard/PayPal, etc). Since the proceeds of sales are stored in your Etsy account, you can help to reduce this cost by cutting down on the frequency of withdrawal from your Etsy account and choosing a cheaper withdrawal option.

## Business sustainability and growth prospects on Etsy

Unless you are on Etsy for a one-off sale or occasional sale, you would be concerned as to how sustainable your business will be on Etsy. You would like to know how long your shop can remain open when your "lease" expires. Luckily, so long as you do not violate the rules of Etsy marketplace, your "lease" on Etsy cannot expire. The only thing that you would need to renew once every four months is your listing which is charged $0.20 for four months.

The other factor that will determine your business sustainability and growth prospects on Etsy is your product's profitability. If you are struggling to make profits or not making a profit at all despite your best effort, then, the business is not sustainable and growth prospects are dim. However, sustainability and growth prospects depend solely on your entrepreneurial acumen rather than Etsy platform or marketplace.

# HOW TO OPEN AN ETSY STOREFRONT

Opening an Etsy storefront is easy. The following are the main steps to opening your Etsy storefront:

1. Gather sufficient information about Etsy
2. Open an account
3. Open your shop
4. Start marketing
5. Run your shop
6. Create and expand your community

**Gather sufficient information about Etsy**

1. Go to "About Us" section of Etsy and read more about this platform and its marketplace. You could get a good gem of information.
2. Check on Etsy policies. The policies are extremely important for you to understand so that you do not inadvertently violate them.
3. Review Etsy Sellers' fee to be sure that they fit your business expectations. We have already covered the fees but be sure to read so that you can get the latest update.

**Open your Etsy account**

To be able to sell or buy items on Etsy, you first need to be an account holder on Etsy. To open an account on Etsy:

1. Click on 'Register' button on the top-left side of the Home Page
2. Fill-in registration details in the pop-up dialog box that appears
3. Create your profile.

**Open your Etsy Shop**

Once you are comfortable that you are well informed and ready to do business on Etsy, the next logical move is to open your Etsy account.

The following steps will enable you to open Etsy account:

1. Click on <u>Sell on Etsy</u> button at the top-right corner of the Home page. A new page will appear with 'Open a Shop' button almost in the middle. Click on it to open your shop.
2. In the dialog box that appears after the click, fill-in details of your preferred shop language, country, and currency.
3. Name your shop.

4. Create your first listing (product) that meets Etsy's <u>market rules</u>.
5. Choose the mode of payment from your customers.
6. Provide details of your billing information.

After successfully following these steps, your Etsy shop is set. The next thing is to enhance it so that it can be ready for business.

**Enhancing your shop**

Once you have opened your shop, the next stage is to enhance it so that it can be ready for public launch.

The following steps will help you enhance your shop:

1. Craft your shop policy details
2. Add your shop cover photo plus icon
3. Add an 'About' section to your shop
4. Arrange your shop items using Shop Organizer in the Shop Section

You can always add more listings to your shop using listings manager.

**Start marketing**

Once you are done with enhancing your shop, you can now comfortably launch it and start marketing.

The following are some of the things you need to do to ensure effective marketing:

1. Optimize your listing's searchability on Etsy (Etsy's SEO)
2. Promote your listing to potential buyers on Etsy marketplace by offering enticements
3. Advertise
4. Establish a physical presence in craft market fairs so that you can be able to dish out your shop contacts, and if possible, sell.

**Run your shop**

With customers starting to troop into your shop, you are now in a higher gear. The following are things that you will need to do so that running your shop become more productive:

- Provide a great service
- Analyze your buyer behavior and make necessary adjustments
- Increase your listing based on new findings from your analysis of customer behavior
- Increase your marketing effort through promotion and publicity

## Create and expand your community

It is from desire that you get customers. The greatest work is how to convert members of your community into customers. However, the smaller your community the lower is the potential for your customers. Thus, the first task is to create and expand your community.

While the Etsy ecosystem already has a community, you should not just focus on it. You have to go far and beyond. The following are potential sources for recruiting members into your community:

- Etsy ecosystem
- Social media
- Your website and blog
- Your offline shop

## Social media

Apart from the already existing Etsy community, social media is the most impactful source of recruiting community members. The most potential social media platforms for your recruitment are:

1. Pinterest
2. Facebook
3. Twitter

4. Instagram

## Your website/blog

It is great to open up a website or blog for your shop. To make this a great success:

- Include your shop name in your domain name
- Brand your website with the same theme as your shop
- Create a page with listing mirroring that on Etsy with links to your Etsy shop
- Use blog to talk more about your listing and engage your audience on your blog
- Create a tweetable title for your blog post and blog content that can be posted on Facebook
- Post your image on Pinterest/Instagram and embed it into your blog

## Your offline shop

Having a storefront on Etsy does not stop you from having a brick-and-mortar storefront. If you have time and money to have an offline shop, do it. This storefront can help you offer an opportunity to those who visit it to be redirected to your online storefront if they don't buy the item straight away.

# BEST PRODUCTS TO SELL ON ETSY

To succeed on Etsy marketplace, it is important to have the right products that meet the needs of your target buyers. You must be able to have the right product idea in order to create it and stock in your shop. Before you go down to product ideas, you need to work out your niche so that within it you can be able to focus your ideas thus avoiding a wild goose chase.

## Selecting your niche

With products ideas in mind, it is easy to narrow down to exactly what fits on Etsy marketplace in terms of categorization/inches.

The following are the main niches/categories on Etsy:

1. Jewelry
2. Women
3. Men
4. Art
5. Vintage
6. Gift Ideas
7. Trending Items

8. Kids

9. Mobile accessories

10. Home and Living

11. Crafts supplies

## Potential sources of product ideas

The following are potential sources from which to scout for product ideas:

- Online crafts marketplaces – Although there are fewer crafts-only marketplaces, it is good to visit those that have a special place allocated to craft items. Amazon and eBay have such places. Analyzing them and determining which kind of item is in high demand and comparing the same to what is in high demand on Etsy plus what fetches better prices, would enable you to have ideas for your product. Remember, you are not only attracting existing customers on Etsy's marketplace, but you are also pooling others across the world.

- Trade fairs – Visit trade fairs where handicrafts are shown. Observe customer interests at such trade fairs for tips on what sells most. You can also pose as a customer to inquire and know more about how the exhibitionists are handling potential customers and squeeze out potential leads that can help you in future should you reach a point where you need to scale-up and diversify your channels.

- Travel sites - Visiting travel blogs to find out tourist sentiments about craft souvenirs and inquiring from them why they bought the kind of crafts that they bought can help you enter this special niche.

- Travelling – Travel to places where most buyers of crafts come from. This way you should be able to get first-hand information about their unique tastes and preferences. It is good to visit travel site blogs to find hints about places to travel to.

- Antique auction sites – If you have interest in dealing with vintages, it will be great to visit antique auction sites/markets to explore those vintages/antiques that attracts higher price and be able to understand buyer preference.

**Narrowing down to what to sell on Etsy**

After doing your own research, you can match your findings with information available about Etsy's bestseller. What you must not forget is that you have to balance your skills, passion, and demand. You do not have to go for an item simply because it is the bestseller.

The following are the Top 10 Bestsellers on Etsy:

1. Stickers
2. Handmade Kids clothing
3. Homemade candies
4. Party decorations
5. Vinyl and Heat-transfer supplies
6. Jewelry articles and findings
7. Home décor, art, and collectibles
8. Unique items
9. Vintages
10. Hard-to-find items

# MARKETING ON ETSY

To be able to have an in-depth understanding of what social media marketing is all about; we must first understand what marketing is all about.

**What is marketing?**

Marketing is a social process involving creation and exchange of value with an aim of satisfying needs and wants.

In this process, the creators of value (sellers) are rewarded by the consumers of value (buyers). The consumers receive a need-satisfying product while the sellers get the price (reward).

In marketing, a product is not necessarily a good or a service but a combination of all processes and activities undertaken to deliver need-satisfaction. Communication is part of this need-satisfaction. Engagement is part of this need-satisfaction. Content that informs and inspires Goodwill is part of this need-satisfaction.

**Needs vs. Wants**

A need is an intrinsic worth in a product that provides a solution to a consumer. On the other hand, a want is a desire for a need. This desire may take a different form than the need itself. For example, the want for sugar may satisfy the desire to have a sweet taste. However, there is an inherent need that may not necessarily be apparent to the one who has the desire. The need is the instant energy provided by sugar. Thus, a consumer may have craving for sugar and only gets satisfied once this inherent need is addressed.

As a marketer, you have to go beyond the want and reach out to the need. Once you identify the need, you can easily create different products that appeal to different tastes of desires. If you do not identify the need, you may end up erroneously misinterpreting consumer desires and come up with a product that will not satisfy their needs.

For a solution to satisfy wants, it must have utility. The key objective of the market mix is to enhance the utility of a given solution.

**Utility**

Utility refers to the ability of a product/solution to meet customer's wants. There are six key utilities:

1. Form utility – Satisfaction obtained when a solution is delivered in the right consumable form.

2. Time utility - Satisfaction derived from a solution being delivered at the right time.

3. Place utility - Satisfaction derived from a solution being delivered at the right place.

4. Possession utility - Satisfaction derived from a solution from one being able to enjoy the right to possess it. This utility may be granted in the form of license, free delivery, fast installation, follow-up service, etc.

5. Information utility - Satisfaction derived from customers being able to have sufficient information to make the right decision.

6. Service utility - Satisfaction derived from customers being able to enjoy fast, friendly and useful service. This may include both pre-sale, on-sale and after-sale service.

**Market mix**

A market mix is a combination of key ingredients in a marketing policy that seeks to deliver a need-satisfying product.

To be able to address the needs of consumers, you have to embrace a customer-focused orientation. A market mix for customer-focused orientation comprises of Solution, Information, Value, and Access (SIVA)

- Solution - This is a product that matches the need of a customer. It answers the following questions; what is it? What problem does it solve?
- Information - Refers to promotional activities aimed at creating customer awareness, trigger desire and necessitate purchase decision. It answers the following question; why is this solution for me? How do I use it? When do I use it? What more do I need to know?
- Value – This is the quality of satisfaction gain in the exchange process. The customer gets satisfied with the product while the seller gets satisfied with the price. It answers the following questions; what is in it for me? How do I benefit?
- Access – This is about delivery. For a product to satisfy a customer, it must be delivered or accessible. This means that it must be conveniently within customer's reach. How can I have it?

**Applying marketing concept to your Etsy business**

Craft and artistic work has a lot of sentimental value. Thus, your creative product should be able to manifest solution in the consumer's psychology. Without even words, the design should be able to communicate its need-satisfying proposition. The buyer should see his/her unique need being satisfied. It should be able to indicate subtly the problem that is being solved. Some of these needs/ "problems" are:

- The desire for unique identity – Most of those who shop for handmade crafts want a unique item that they can identify with. There is a hidden desire to satisfy an identity ego. You should be able to understand your buyer persona and identify this ego.
- The desire for authenticity – Handmade crafts such as jewelry, artistic drawing, etc, are bought mainly for their authentic purposes. The buyer wants originality. The buyer wants a story to tell about this authentic piece of craft. If a buyer has a desire for uniqueness and authenticity, then, the buyer would be willing to pay a higher price just to achieve this.
- The desire for memorable attachment - This is the desire that makes people buy souvenirs and gifts.
- The desire for comfort – when it comes to handmade fabrics, the greatest desire is often comfort. Thus, your product must manifest this solution in the buyer's psychology.
- The desire for durability – Buyers wants artistic drawings that can last. Thus, the paint used should be durable. It

should not be such easy to react to exposure to light, moisture, etc. When it comes to furniture, it should not easily break.

- The desire for functionality – The product should be fit for purpose. When it comes to furniture, there are those buyers who are looking for a piece of furniture that is highly portable and detachable. This is the solution that you should put forward.

- The desire for safety – If a bed or chair breaks, it is likely to injure the users. Thus, buyers would be concerned about how safe it is to use such. Safety also applies to homemade cosmetics, foodstuff, recipes, etc. For those products which safety is a priority, you have to emphasize on how your product solves this concern.

**Provide information**

While the product speaks for itself, it cannot say it all. You have to add informational value beyond that which is visible to the buyer. Most buyers want to identify with the product's creator – the solution provider. Information helps to enhance the value of the solution.

You have to provide information in such a manner that taps into the inner desire of your buyer persona. There is a great sentimental value when it comes to crafts and artistic creations. This information should include:

What makes your craft stand out? – In this case, describe the product's intrinsic and extrinsic qualities. Intrinsic qualities include the quality of the material used, the expertise of the creator, the unique creation process, etc.

How would the buyer use it? – Some products do not have a discernible usage at first sight. Thus, you would need to provide the buyer with the potential and alternative usage of such a product.

**Justify the value**

Many times, marketers fail to beat the competition due to lack of value proposition. One marketer can sell twice the quantity of the same product at double the price compared to another marketer. The difference lies in how a marketer makes the value proposition. Cutting down the price does not necessarily increase sales. Even if it does, obviously, it cuts on your profits and eventually your wealth potential. Thus, you have to spend more time on creating a value proposition that inspires the buyer to open up his/her wallet and make a buy decision.

The following are some of the ways by which you can justify the value:

- Expound on the product's **uniqueness**
- Show how **authentic your** product is

- Highlight features that make your product **comfortable** to use

## Branding your products/shop

This involves creating brand identity, brand value, brand deliverability, and brand recognition, among others.

## Brand identity (shop)

Brand identity is about differentiating your brand from others. The following are things you need to do in order to have a brand identity:

- Create your shop's brand name– The brand name should relate to your niche rather than your product. If your niche is jewelry, let your brand name pronounce it clearly.

- Create logo – A logo creates a unique impression in the mind of the buyer thus enabling the buyer to easily identify your products and distinguish them competitors' products

- Create trademark – A trademark is simply a unique mark that identifies a particular product.

- Create a package design – A package design for your product helps to enhance your brand recognition at the delivery point. Buyers are able to know quickly that the product is from you. This helps to minimize buyer remorse.

## Specifications:

- Shop title – limited to 55 characters
- Cover photo – minimum 1200px x 300px
- Shop logo – minimum 500px x 500px
- Featured listings – these are items that will feature on your shop's homepage.
- Shop announcement – This is a special announcement to the public about your shop.

## Brand value/measurability (price)

Pricing depends on the buyer's perceived value. Some products fetch a higher price than others despite having the same intrinsic value. This is because how the seller has managed to create an impression in the buyers' minds about their higher value.

## Brand deliverability (place)

Consumers get satisfaction when a brand is within reach of meeting their needs and wants. The channels of distribution and delivery time are unique attributes that can distinguish a brand from the rest.

# Brand recognition (promotion)

Brand recognition refers to activities and processes engaged in making the brand get recognized by target customers. Brand recognition involves publicity and promotion.

## Publicity

- Niche website
- Press releases
- Public relations
- Advertisement
- Product/niche directory listing

## Promotion

- Free samples
- Gifts
- Free eBooks
- Free user training

## Brand sensitivity (people)

- Train customer service representatives to deliver great service
- Interact via social media

- Respond to feedback

- Factor in consumer psychology

**Brand activity (process)**

- Productivity

- Economy (efficiency and effectiveness)

- Turnover

**Brand performance (performance)**

- Performance measurement – infographics

- Consumer satisfaction

- Market response (recognition and improved sales)

- Customer loyalty (Goodwill)

- Customer reviews

- Profitability

**How to optimize your listing**

Keyword optimization is extremely critical to the performance of your listing on Etsy. It will determine how much traffic flows to your shop and thus of this traffic, you are capable of converting.

To optimize your keywords, you have to factor the following:

1. Understanding of Etsy's search algorithm

2. Keyword research

3. Click-Through Rate (CTR) factors

4. Conversion rate factors

5. Sales as an optimization factor

**Understanding Etsy's Algorithm**

To optimize an engine, you have to master how it operates. This is the same rationale for Search Engine Optimization (SEO). Etsy's Search Engine has a unique algorithm that helps buyers to find quickly the products that they need from its marketplace. Though Etsy's algorithm remains secret, there are many hints that give a clue to the key factors. With an understanding of the key factors, you can find and use keywords that can optimize your listing's SEO. This will put you one step ahead of the pack.

Your effort should be geared towards your listing/products appearing on the first SERP. If it can appear among the top-three items, there is a great likelihood that the link leading to your listing will be clicked.

The following are the key factors are considered by Etsy's search engine algorithm when it comes to ranking:

- **Relevance factors** – This refers to how well the product listing matches the search query. Relevance is mainly computed based on how the keyword is used and how it is positioned (e.g. in the product's name, product description, etc)

- **Performance factors** – This refers to how the product has performed in terms of popularity and success. The three critical performance indicators are; Click-Through Rate (CTR), Conversion Rate (CR) and Sales Turnover (ST). Of course, the most rational ranking priority is ST followed by CR and finally CTR. However, it is CTR that gives birth to CR. CR boosts the chances of ST occurring or increasing. It is also important to note that CTR depends heavily on relevance factors (Etsy SEO).

It is important to observe that relevance factors (which are mostly within your control and which you can greatly influence through SEO) directly and indirectly drive performance factors (which you may not have great leeway to influence). Nonetheless, product quality, branding, pricing, promotion and customer support are factors which are within your control and which you can tune to greatly improve your performance and drive ST.

# How to carry out thorough keyword research

Keyword research (KR) is the bedrock of SEO. Without KR, your SEO effort is a blind, primitive guesswork. What is keyword research? Keyword research involves finding all relevant keywords for your product that would enable it to be easily searchable. The most important approach in keyword research is to put yourself in the customer's shoes. In this regard, you ask yourself, "Which kind of words would I type on the search bar if I wanted to find a certain kind of product that I need? Thus, SEO keywords are simply keywords that a customer would most likely use to search for your product.

## Types of keywords

There are two main types of keywords:

- Short-tail keywords

- Long-tail keywords

## Short-tail keywords

Also known as "head" or "term" keywords, they comprise of 1 to 3 words. There are two types of short-tail keywords:

- Primary keywords – These keywords are specific to the product's core essence. This includes its identification and description, for example, "jogging shoes".

- Secondary keywords – These are keywords that associate the primary keywords to a target group, event, season, time, circumstance/situation, function, size, shape, appearance, material, place, etc. For example, secondary keywords associated with "handmade cardigans" could be; target group: "children handmade cardigans", "male handmade cardigans", "female handmade cardigans"; event: "Halloween handmade cardigans"; season: "winter handmade cardigans", etc.

**Long-tail keywords**

Long-tail keywords are those keywords (usually three or more words) that are more specific to meeting a certain need or providing a certain solution.

SEO features of long-tail keywords:

- They have low competition

- They have a low search rate

Advantages of long-tail keywords

- They have high conversion rate – Most serious searchers are specific about what they are looking for and thus they are more likely to buy an item should they find it. For example, if you are selling tour packages for Mount Everest then "Mount Everest" will bring over 1000 visitors per day. However, most of the visitors probably are geography students or those who just want to get general information about Mount Everest. Very few are interested in tour package – probably 5. On the other hand, if you use "Mount Everest climbing tour package", only serious persons would type such on their search bar. Probably, out of 80 visitors, 15 of them will buy the package. Thus, though there is less competition for long-tail keywords (low search rate) there is higher conversion rate.

- Since long-tail keywords have less competition, their CPC (Cost per Click) rate is low. This means that you will use less advertising budget.

**Click-Through Rate (CTR) factors**

Click-Through Rate refers to the ratio of the number of people who click on an advert against the number of people who view the advert.

Factors determining Click-Through Rate are:

- Brand name – An attractive brand name will more likely excite a potential customer to click so as to know what the brand is all about

- Title – A great title will compel a potential customer to want to know what your product is all about

- Image – An optimized image creates a great impression about a product thus raising interest and curiosity

- Price – A price that seems too good will raise potential customer's curiosity to find out more

**Conversion Rate factors**

Conversion refers to the act of converting site visitors into buying customers. Conversion rate refers to the number of conversions per click (ad click). The conversion rate is computed by dividing the number of conversions against the number of clicks.

The following are key factors that determine conversion rate:

- Image – An optimized image creates an impression about your product's quality, need-satisfaction, and fitness for purpose among other impressions that compel a potential customer to try your product.

- Reviews – Reviews are about reputation. Positive reviews increase your product reputation. Thus, a potential customer asks "if all these customers are happy and satisfied about this product, why not me?" This boosts the customer's confidence to buy your product.

- Description format – When it comes to description, it is not just a matter of compelling description but also presentation. Many customers are easily worn out after going through dozens of listings to arrive at your listing. A poor presentation will discourage them from reading your description; hence fail to buy your product. A bullet point presentation makes it easy for a customer to read as the key points are summarized. This too motivates a quick buying decision.

## How to optimize your listing content

You have to do keyword optimization of every part of your listing content including title, price (captured by Etsy price metrics), photos, product description, search terms (most likely used by buyers to search for items).

## Optimizing listing title

To optimize your title, it should:

- Be less than 55 characters

- Concisely describe your product

- Be grammatically correct

- Contain your brand name

- SEO optimized

## Optimizing price

To optimize price:

- Set a price that would attract potential buyers away from your competitors, yet leaves you with a sustainable profit margin.

## Optimizing photos

- Save using names with SEO keywords but each photo must have a unique name

## Optimizing Product description:

1. Incorporate both short-tail and long-tail keywords

2. Consider applying for Etsy's Enhanced Brand Content

## Optimizing Search Terms:

- Use secondary keywords – at least 5 of them

## Optimizing via Keywords from Etsy's PPC

- Etsy has a provision for PPC. Take advantage of it to boost your presence and traffic flow.

# SCALING UP YOUR ETSY BUSINESS

Scaling up your Etsy business simply means increasing sales in both quantity and value. It also means expanding your sales channels.

The following are the fundamental things that you will need to do in order to scale up your Etsy business:

1. Increase your productivity
2. Expand your market
3. Streamline your production process
4. Streamline your supply process
5. Carry out enterprise-wide scaling

## Increase your personal productivity

Etsy is about creativity. It is not about mass manufacturing venture. Thus, it will largely involve your hands-on effort, especially at the initial stages. This is where personal productivity comes in handy. To increase your personal productivity:

- Put more emphasis on creativity and innovation
- Be less activity-oriented and more result-oriented

- Increase your time-value

## Expand your market

To increase sales, you have to expand your market. To expand your market, you will need to do the following:

- Diversify your niches
- Diversify your product portfolio
- Increase your channels/marketplaces
- Increase traffic/exposure to your shop
- Boost engagement
- Advertise
- Blog
- Offer gifts to loyal customers
- Video demos
- Offer training and other ancillary services

## Increase traffic/exposure to your shop (to customize and summarize)

Your listing is like a center and Etsy the city within which that center is found. There are many channels flowing into and through Etsy and some of them to your center. To increase the traffic flow to your center, you have to create more feeder channels from the main channels into your center. This is where Etsy SEO comes in. However, this is simply the inner traffic.

Thus, how much traffic will flow into your center will depend on the inner traffic. What if the existing inner traffic is not sufficient?

If the inner traffic is not sufficient, then, you will have to attract outer traffic into the inner traffic. This traffic will come from sources outside Etsy ecosystem. Hence, we have two main sources of traffic to your listing:

- Etsy ecosystem

- Beyond Etsy ecosystem

Driving traffic from Etsy ecosystem into your listing encompasses the following:

- Etsy SEO – We have already covered this under Keyword optimization of your listing

- Focus on getting quality positive reviews (through promotion, great product, and service) – Positive reviews are largely related to successful sales and great customer experience. They are a premium quality of your sales turnover (ST). The higher the volume of positive reviews the greater is the performance of your listing.

**Driving traffic beyond Etsy ecosystem into your listing**

The following are ways by which you can drive traffic from beyond Etsy ecosystem:

- Non-Etsy SEO – Driving traffic from beyond Etsy will require you to device a different approach to SEO targeting popular search engines including Google, Bing, Yahoo, among others. This is mainly done through content marketing.

- Directory listing – There are many directories offering niche placements and contact details. Providing these with links to your Etsy listing page is the best way to utilize directory listing to drive traffic to your listing.

- Social Media activity – It is estimated that over 2 billion people are active on social media. Thus, using social media can be a great means of driving traffic to your listing. For example, you can open a Facebook page for your niche and post content with links to your Etsy listing. You can use Twitter to provide news about your new product launch or enhanced features or versions of your existing product. You can use Pinterest to show photos of your newly launched products. StumbleUpon is a great social media for new product discovery. You simply do not forget to link your social media activity to your Etsy listing.

- Videos – Videos have become the most magnetic attraction of millennial generation. If your products are targeting millennials, then, creating "how-to" videos is the best way to attract them to your Etsy listing. Make a great "how-to" video about your product, upload on YouTube and simply link it to your Etsy listing.

- Press Releases (PR) – There are several PR sites where you can launch your press release. Though reputable PR sites are difficult to list on (due to the high standard of quality expected), once successful, you can get a huge volume of traffic to your site.

- Advertisement (PPC) – Pay per Click (PPC) is the most popular form of online advertising. The Google empire is heavily reliant on PPC advertisement. Facebook too offers PPC advertisement. There are many others, but these are the leaders. Simply create an advert (text, image, animation, video or a combination of some or all of these) as per the advertising platform requirements. Pay and upload the advert and let the advertising platform launch it to your target audience. Whenever potential customers click the advert, they are directed to your product listing.

- Niche Website – A niche website is a website specifically designed and developed to provide content and promote activities related to your niche products. This is a must-have if your intent is to increase your income.

**Advantages of owning niche website as a tool for driving traffic**

Niche website has advantages over other advertising media discussed above. The following are some of the advantages:

- It is cheaper in the long-term – Once you have created a niche website, all you need to pay is hosting. If you are not busy, you can easily run your niche website, more so, if it is a CMS (Content Management System) such as WordPress, Drupal, Joomla, among others. So far, WordPress is the most popular CMS to use to develop your niche website. It is so simple such that you can actually build it yourself.

- You own your content – When it comes to online marketing, content is king. To own your content, you have to self-host your niche website. There are plenty of online platforms where you can post your content. These include Blogger, WordPress.org (as opposed to WordPress.com), among others, which provide you with a website where you load content. You do not spend money to create the website and neither do you spend money to host it. It is "free!" Really? In the real sense, there is a pay – your content. When you provide your content to such "free" websites, you forfeit your right to it. The content ceases to belong to you. The provider of this "free" website uses it as a source of advertisement revenue – earning at your sacrifice!

- You can optimize on structural SEO – SEO is not just about content. It is also about the "container" that holds the content and channels (links) that draw out information from it. SEO-friendly programming requires that you use a programming language that is friendly to search engines (such as HTML) as opposed to a programming language that is not SEO-friendly (such as JavaScript). Links to content should also flow without breakage (or obstruction) so that the content can easily be accessed, flow and be fetched by the search engines. Links are broken when they are not associated with any content (i.e. linked to a deleted page, removed the video, removed page, etc). Links are obstructed if the search engines cannot access the content being linked to (due to the usage of non-SEO-friendly language). Having pages that are not linked creates redundant inaccessible "islands" of content.

- You can place your own advertisements on the website for free – You do not have to pay anyone to advertise on your niche website. Etsy has widgets that enable you to advertise products (including your products) on your website.

- You can advertise your website just as you would advertise your product – Your content is a product! The more it is consumed the more likely its consumers will be interested in consuming what it refers to – your products. Thus, it makes great sense to advertise your niche website.

- You can provide more information on your niche website about your product, which you could not provide in your listing – Unlike your listing on Etsy; there is no space limitation when it comes to your niche website. You can give detailed product features, user instructions, demonstration videos, animation graphics, offer promotional materials (downloads, free samples, gifts, etc – which you cannot possibly do on Etsy when you have individual seller plan).

- You can easily market your niche in the listing directories – Most listing directories do not entertain content that solicits customers (i.e. sales pitch content). This makes it impossible to link your Etsy listing on them. However, you can link to your niche site page provided that the link targets content that is not sales-pitched in nature. The good thing is that you can place your adverts on the page just as Google and other advertising media do.

**Getting initial reviews**

Getting initial reviews requires good work. There are no tricks to getting genuine positive reviews for your product.

The following are some of the things that can bring forth initial positive reviews

- Great listing – A listing that is professional (good photo, proper title, helpful description, etc) will create a positive impression in the customers' mind and will obviously prompt for a reward in terms of a positive review.

- Product quality – Quality product means customer satisfaction. Make sure that the product is of good quality but also meets customers' expectations as described. Thus, do not exaggerate customer expectations. Be honest with what the customer is expected to get.

- Proper pricing – Price represents the sacrifice that the customer makes to receive the value of your product. If the customer feels that the sacrifice (price) is abnormally higher than the value (product quality), then, negative reviews are likely. However, if customers are satisfied that they have received value for their money, then, positive reviews are more likely.

- Good inventory management – There is nothing frustrating like when customers miss product they want due to stock-outs. This will negate their goodwill and thus reduce the likelihood of a 5-star review. Ensuring that product is available when needed is improves customer satisfaction. This can be achieved through good inventory management.

**Streamline your production process**

- Increase efficiency

**Streamline your inventory supply process**

- Fulfillment (e.g. shipbob)
- Automate inventory management

Fulfillment

The term 'Fulfillment' is commonly used in merchandise business by vendors when it comes to dealing with orders. The Order is either 'fulfilled' or 'unfulfilled'. A fulfilled Order is a one where the goods are delivered as per the Order and all its terms met including invoicing, billing and payment. Unfulfilled Order is an order that has not yet been acted upon or it is not completed.

Thus, in a more technical sense, fulfillment can be defined as the whole process of receiving, packaging and delivering as per the Order.

Fulfillment is commonly applied in e-commerce.

**Why outsource fulfillment?**

Like any other service that one outsources, the following are basic guiding criteria for outsourcing fulfillment service:

- When it becomes more expensive to render the service in-house.

- When it becomes more productive to focus on the core functions and thus the need to outsource non-core functions.

- When the level of expertise required to render the service is such complex that it cannot be economically met in-house.

- When the scale of operation is such huge to be met in-house e.g. international delivery networks that require extensive logistics infrastructure.

## What does an ordinary fulfillment entail?

Basically, fulfillment, though depends on custom contractual terms, encompasses the following;

- Warehousing (storage of goods)

- Order processing (including re-ordering)

- Delivery (including shipping)

- Returns and exchanges

However, fulfillment can be end-to-end, meaning that the fulfillment company carries out entire process. In addition to the above processes, an end-to-end fulfillment has the following:

- Billing

- Payment processing (Credit-card)

- Call-center services (customer service support)

## Carry out enterprise-wide scaling

- Establish partnerships

- Boost funding options
- Automate your service and production process

# ETSY BUSINESS AUTOMATION

Automating Etsy business process is the best way you can boost your incomes and profits. There is a limit as to how much you can achieve on your own without automation. When you automate your business process, you are able to raise it above your own personal limitations such as fatigue, monotony, sickness, rest and sleep, among others.

The following are some of the key benefits of automation:

- Ability to scale up
- Unlimited possibilities for expansion
- Focus on creativity
- Increased passive income

**Processes that you can automate**

The following are the processes that you can easily automate and whose automation tools we are going to discuss:

- Listing – Listing is more about stocking and presenting your merchandise to the Etsy marketplace. Like any traditional brick-and-mortar shop, the importance of organized attention-capturing display cannot be forsaken. What captures customers' attention attracts money. However great your product is, a poor listing will repel money away thus frustrating your income streams. Listing tools are great for helping you have the best listing possible.

- Inventory management – Having excessive or redundant stock ties your capital thus limiting your income generating options. On the other hand, stock-outs due to inadequate inventory makes you miss on potential incomes, frustrate your customers and attracts negative Goodwill. Having no stock is the other language for telling a potential customer "I don't need your money now, please try elsewhere". The best trick is to have an optimal stock level. However, in a huge, delicate and dynamic market such as Etsy marketplace, you cannot be certain about the most optimal stock level as the market dynamics are extremely fluid. Thus, you need inventory management tools that are critically sensitive and respond efficiently and effectively to the rapidly changing dynamics. At the bare minimum, such tools should be able to forecast the market, predict scenarios, determine minimum stock level, re-order level, re-order quantity and maximum stock level as per the forecast and most likely scenario.

- Consumer insight (consumer metrics) – Big data has become the inevitable reality of global commerce. The volume of data that flows in a day in a global market such as Etsy would require you to employ thousands of pen-and-paper analysts. Luckily, there are big data tools specifically tailored to help you get incisive consumer insights almost instantly. You need to be able to tell consumer trends to be able to forecast changing consumer behavior, attitudes, tastes, and preferences. This is crucial for medium-term and long-term planning. This will greatly help in your product design, product branding, product lifecycle, pricing, inventory management and exploration of new niches.

- Marketing – Marketing is about all efforts geared towards availing need-satisfying/want-satisfying product to the consumer. We have seen its facets (the 8Ps) under 'BRANDING'. It is a massive effort. It is the core consumer-side (as opposed to supplier-side) effort. Whether income streams will flow or not absolutely depends on marketing. This is how critical it is. Thus, marketing tools must not be spared or laid to waste.

- Copywriting and keyword management – Copywriting and keyword management is part of the online marketing strategies. The importance of this unique management continues to grow as we advance in e-commerce. We have seen the importance of keyword optimization before. Here we are looking on how to automate it and available tools that we can use to achieve this automation.

- Customer interaction – We have seen how reviews are important in driving and maintaining traffic (potential income flows) to your listing. However, these reviews depend on how interactive you are with your customers. Building a solid goodwill depends on effective communication. Every customer's action needs a communication response from the seller. With online markets such as Etsy where sales take place 24/7 across the globe, it is not possible to achieve this without the aid of customer interaction tools that detects every customer action and responds appropriately.

## Etsy Business Automation Tools

Etsy has hundreds of business automation tools. We have categorized and hyperlinked some of these tools. You can click each tool to find more about it.

### Theme tools

- Virb
- Etsy Theme Shop
- Etsy App for Facebook
- Merchpin
- IndieMade

### Branding tools

- Vistaprint
- Company Folders

### Etsy Listings Renewal tools

- The Statsy Clockbot
- Best Auto Renew

## Social Media posting

- MySocialPig
- Around.io
- Spreesy
- SocialBoost
- Etsy-fu
- OrangeTwig
- Etsy Items
- Social Rebate
- StoreWoot
- Commonplace
- Etsy Social Shop
- Fanchimp
- PinGroupie
- Bloomberry
- Followercheck
- TwitterAudit

## Social Media Scheduling

- Hootsuite
- Buffer
- Tailwind
- BoardBooster

## Sales/pricing tools

- PriceWoot
- Etsy On Sale
- Seller Tools
- 30-Seconds Catalog Builder
- SalesMap

## Shipping tools

- ShippingEasy
- ShipStation
- Shippo
- ATS International Shipping Tool
- ShipRush
- Shipworks
- ShipSaver
- ShipRobot
- TrueShip
- Shiplark
- 71lbs

- <u>Fitshipper</u>
- <u>eSupplyStore</u>
- <u>Etsy on Sale</u>

## Photography/ Images editing tools

- <u>FotoFuze</u>
- <u>PICT</u>
- <u>Whatify</u>
- <u>Etsy Treasury Slider Widget</u>
- <u>Shoop!</u>
- <u>Picture Flow</u>
- <u>Canva</u>
- <u>Gimp</u>
- <u>PicMonkey</u>
- <u>Compressor</u>
- <u>Blogstomp</u>

## Inventory

- <u>Craftybase</u>
- <u>RunInventory</u>
- <u>SKUlabs</u>
- <u>SynCommerce</u>

- Stitch Labs

## Marketing

- Heartomatic
- Putler
- EtsyMarketingTool
- Etsy Social
- Easy Contests & Promotions Apps
- Shopseen
- EtsySales Map
- Cr8tivity

## Bulk Editing

- Etsy CSV
- ShopShaper
- Zetsy
- Vela
- Nembol

## Accounting toos

- WorkingPoint
- TaxJar
- Unify
- Moneybox.me
- Billbee

- Craft Maker Pro

## Shopping tools

- IFTTT
- Smart Etsy
- ColorMatch
- Etsywishlist
- Scrollsy

## Email Marketing tools

- Mad Mimi
- Etsy Email App
- Respondify
- Drip
- Mailchimp
- Constant Contact

## Time Saver tools

- ShopShaper
- Fulfillrite
- Craftcount
- Craft Maker Pro

## Etsy SEO tools

- Marmalead
- Keyword.io
- Etsy Gadget
- Spacefem's Etsy Tag Analyzer

## Research & Statistics tools

- Craft Count
- Google Shopping Trends
- Google Trends
- Handmade Hunt
- Google Analytics

## Pricing tools

- Flipper Tools – Etsy Sale Price
- Etsy Rank – Profit Calculator
- PriceWoot
- Holiday List
- Etsy Seller Fee Calculator by Craftybase

## Link Shortening tools

- Bit.ly
- Google Link Shortner
- Tiny Url

## Blog Tools

- [Pattern by Etsy](#)
- [InLinkz](#)

## Etsy monitoring tools

- [Etsy Rank – Etsy Market Report](#)
- [Ecommerce Times](#)

- [Etsy Blog](#)

## Vintage Sourcing

- [EstateSales.net](#)
- [YardSales.net](#)
- [Worthpoint](#)

## Fashion trend research tools

- [Polyvore](#)
- [Wanelo](#)
- [Keep](#)
- [Fancy](#)

## Other general utility tools

- <u>Zapier</u>
- <u>Etsy Sales Map</u>
- <u>Trello</u>
- <u>Etsy Rank – Color Trend</u>
- <u>Pantone</u>

## Service automation

So far, we have been discussing more or less on a Do-It-Yourself basis whereby you are mostly a sole proprietor. This is probably the best starting point for a beginner. However, as your business expands and you scale up, you need helping hands. This is whereby you have to automate services that you previously provided by outsourcing them.

The following are services that you can easily outsource:

- Shop Design & Branding

- Listing

- Web design and development

- SEO

- Marketing

- Consumer Metrics

- Customer interactions

You can easily get workers (specialists) to carry out web design, SEO, graphics design (for branding) and marketing from freelancing sites such as Upwork.com, Freelancer.com, Fiverr, among others for a start. If your scale is high, you can enlist the services of established consultants in respective areas.

# CONCLUSION

Thank you for acquiring this book "Etsy: Open an Etsy Storefront and Launch your Handmade Empire".

It is my hope that information provided in this book has inspired your inner entrepreneur and enabled you to dare open an Etsy shop for your handmade crafts and thus begin the journey to building your handmade crafts empire. It is also my sincere hope that you have shared with your friends and loved ones information about this book and encouraged them to acquire a copy for their own reference.

Good luck!

Lightning Source UK Ltd.
Milton Keynes UK
UKHW020640040321
379777UK00010B/650